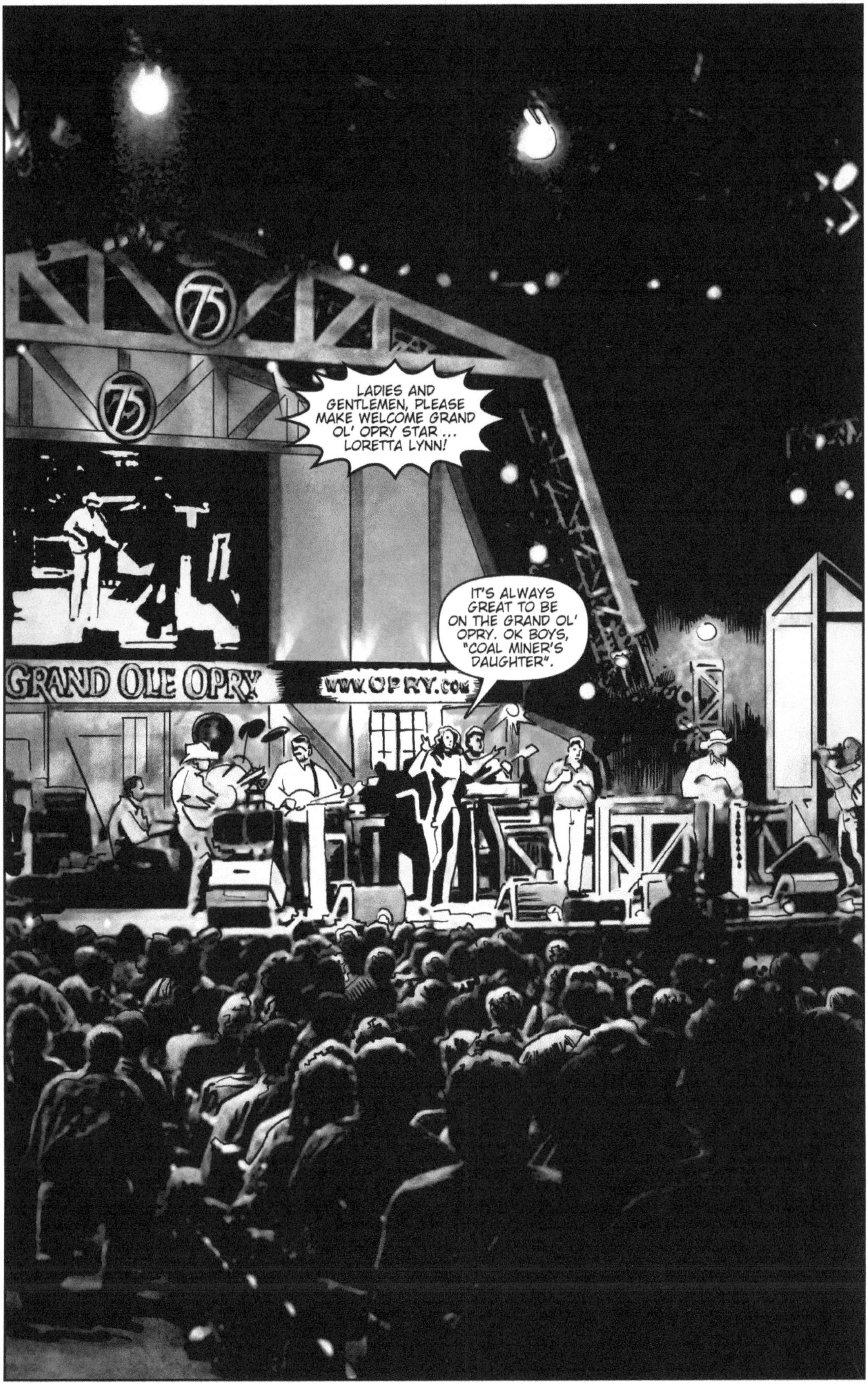
LADIES AND GENTLEMEN, PLEASE MAKE WELCOME GRAND OL' OPRY STAR ... LORETTA LYNN!
GRAND OLE OPRY
WWW.OPRY.COM
IT'S ALWAYS GREAT TO BE ON THE GRAND OL' OPRY. OK BOYS, "COAL MINER'S DAUGHTER".

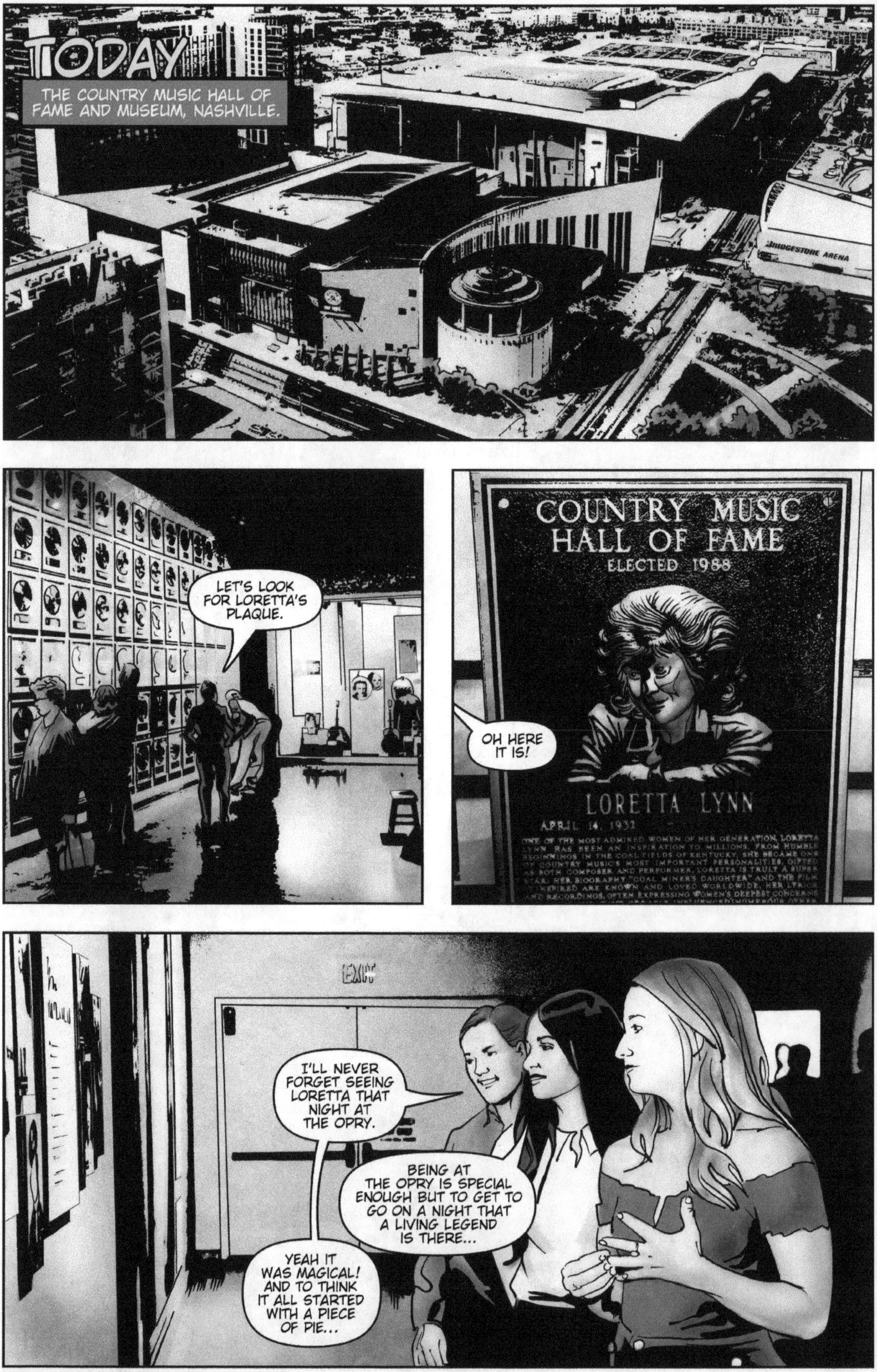

TODAY
THE COUNTRY MUSIC HALL OF FAME AND MUSEUM, NASHVILLE.
BRIDGESTONE ARENA
LET'S LOOK FOR LORETTA'S PLAQUE.
COUNTRY MUSIC HALL OF FAME
ELECTED 1988
OH HERE IT IS!
LORETTA LYNN
APRIL 14, 1932
EXIT
I'LL NEVER FORGET SEEING LORETTA THAT NIGHT AT THE OPRY.
BEING AT THE OPRY IS SPECIAL ENOUGH BUT TO GET TO GO ON A NIGHT THAT A LIVING LEGEND IS THERE...
YEAH IT WAS MAGICAL! AND TO THINK IT ALL STARTED WITH A PIECE OF PIE...

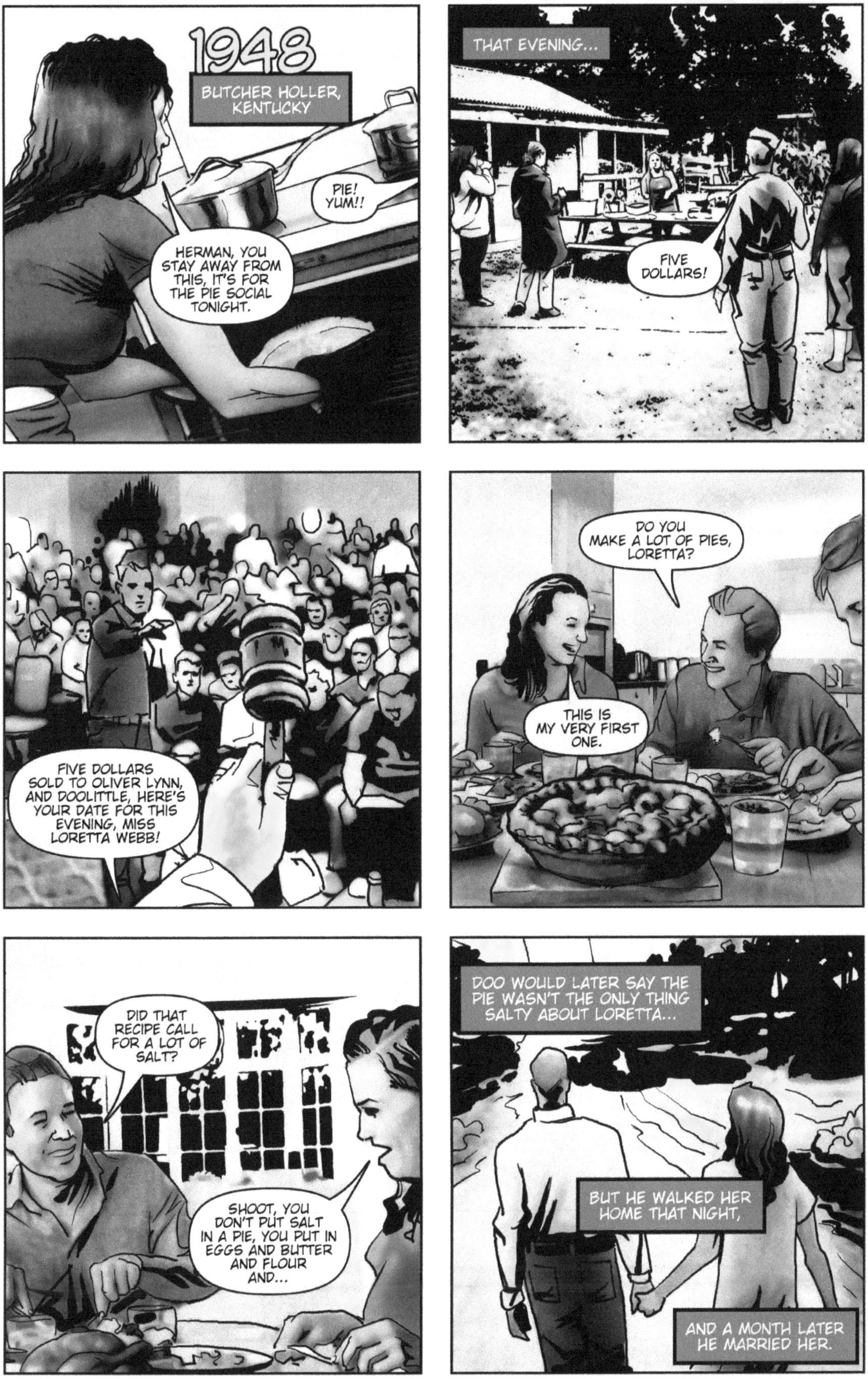
1948
BUTCHER HOLLER, KENTUCKY
PIE! YUM!!
HERMAN, YOU STAY AWAY FROM THIS, IT'S FOR THE PIE SOCIAL TONIGHT.
THAT EVENING...
FIVE DOLLARS!
FIVE DOLLARS SOLD TO OLIVER LYNN, AND DOOLITTLE, HERE'S YOUR DATE FOR THIS EVENING, MISS LORETTA WEBB!
DO YOU MAKE A LOT OF PIES, LORETTA?
THIS IS MY VERY FIRST ONE.
DID THAT RECIPE CALL FOR A LOT OF SALT?
SHOOT, YOU DON'T PUT SALT IN A PIE, YOU PUT IN EGGS AND BUTTER AND FLOUR AND...
DOO WOULD LATER SAY THE PIE WASN'T THE ONLY THING SALTY ABOUT LORETTA...
BUT HE WALKED HER HOME THAT NIGHT,
AND A MONTH LATER HE MARRIED HER.

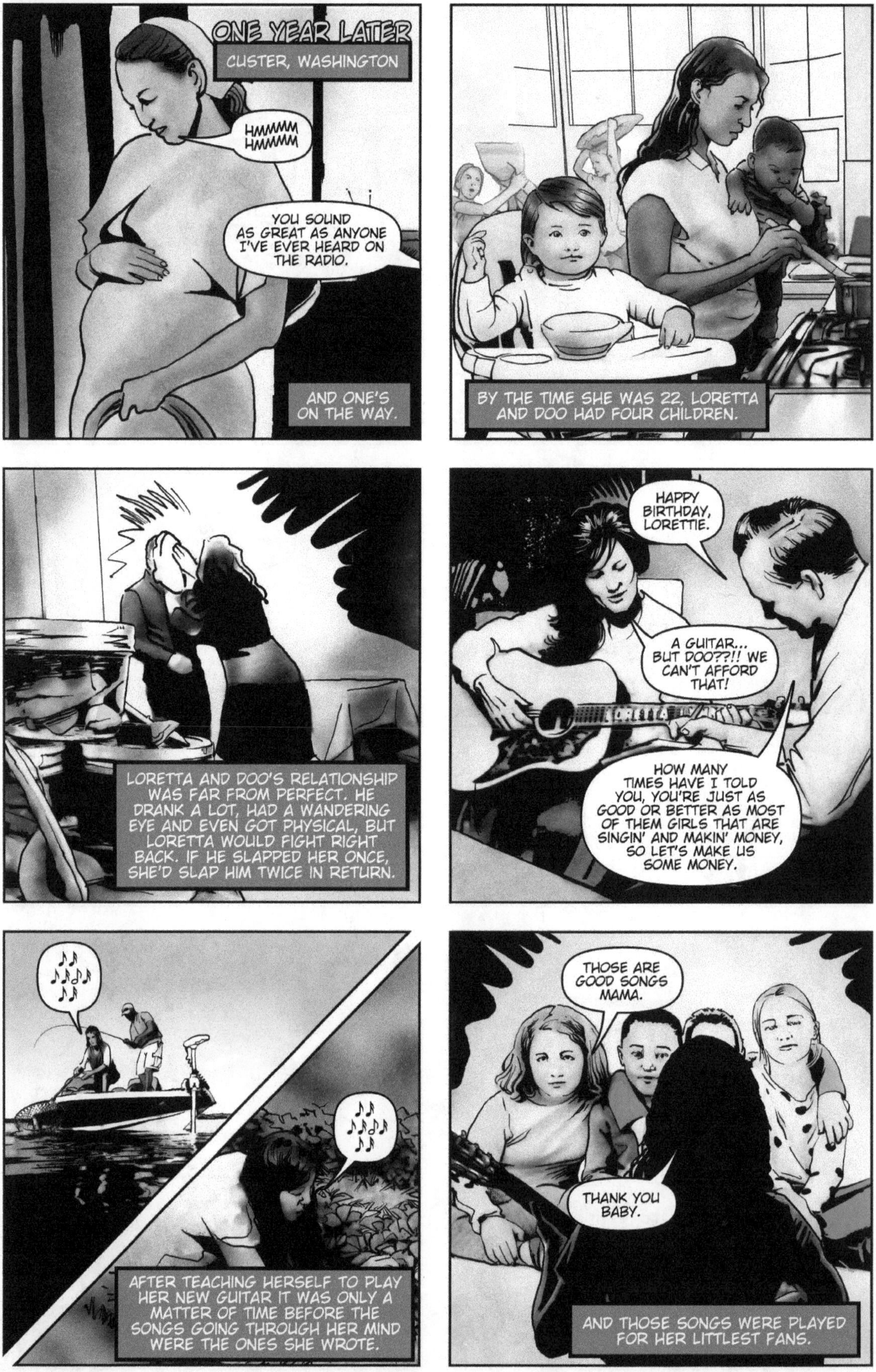
ONE YEAR LATER
CUSTER, WASHINGTON
HMMMM HMMMM
YOU SOUND AS GREAT AS ANYONE I'VE EVER HEARD ON THE RADIO.
AND ONE'S ON THE WAY.
BY THE TIME SHE WAS 22, LORETTA AND DOO HAD FOUR CHILDREN.
LORETTA AND DOO'S RELATIONSHIP WAS FAR FROM PERFECT. HE DRANK A LOT, HAD A WANDERING EYE AND EVEN GOT PHYSICAL, BUT LORETTA WOULD FIGHT RIGHT BACK. IF HE SLAPPED HER ONCE, SHE'D SLAP HIM TWICE IN RETURN.
HAPPY BIRTHDAY, LORETTIE.
A GUITAR... BUT DOO??!! WE CAN'T AFFORD THAT!
HOW MANY TIMES HAVE I TOLD YOU, YOU'RE JUST AS GOOD OR BETTER AS MOST OF THEM GIRLS THAT ARE SINGIN' AND MAKIN' MONEY, SO LET'S MAKE US SOME MONEY.
AFTER TEACHING HERSELF TO PLAY HER NEW GUITAR IT WAS ONLY A MATTER OF TIME BEFORE THE SONGS GOING THROUGH HER MIND WERE THE ONES SHE WROTE.
THOSE ARE GOOD SONGS MAMA.
THANK YOU BABY.
AND THOSE SONGS WERE PLAYED FOR HER LITTLEST FANS.

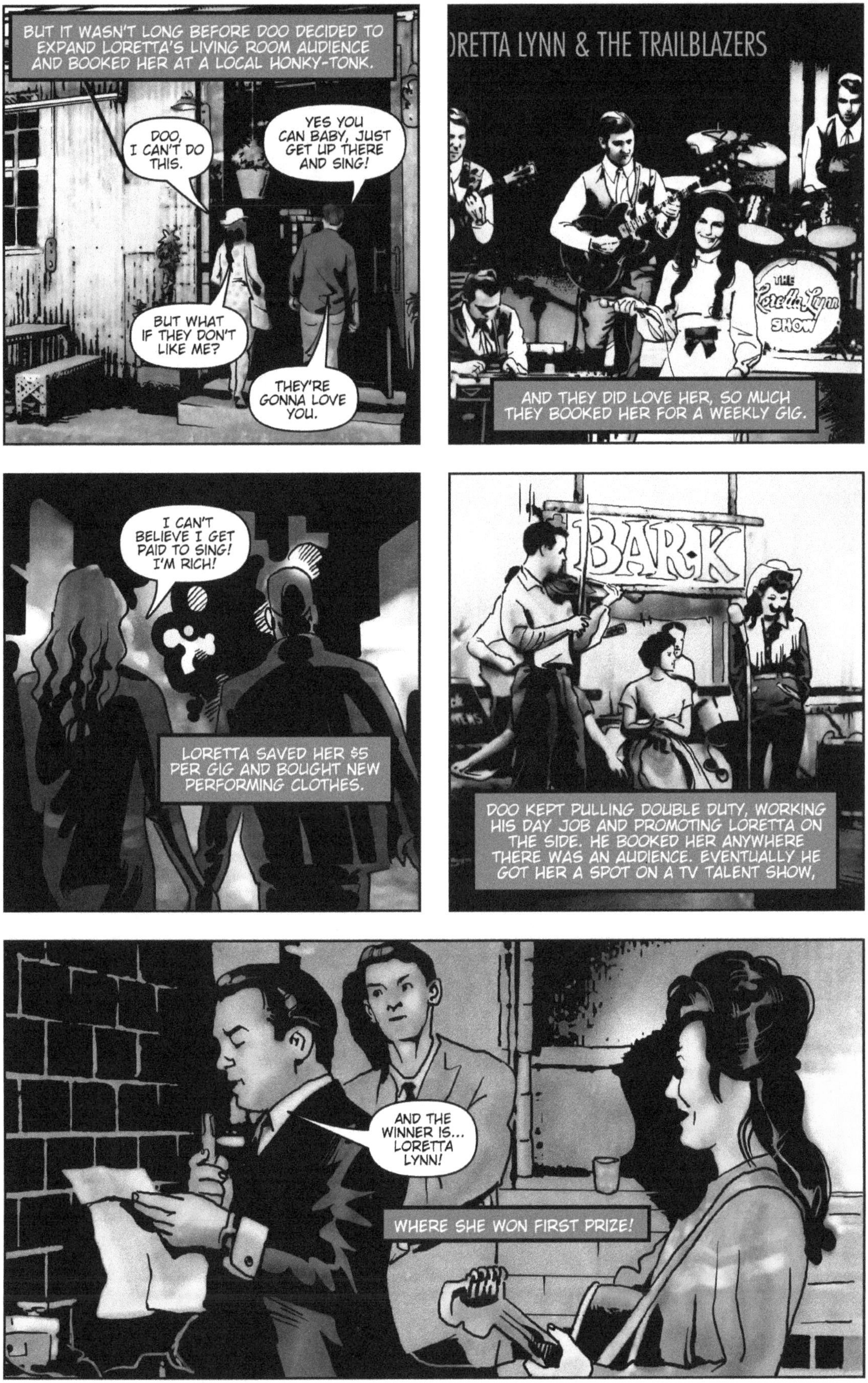
BUT IT WASN'T LONG BEFORE DOO DECIDED TO EXPAND LORETTA'S LIVING ROOM AUDIENCE AND BOOKED HER AT A LOCAL HONKY-TONK.
DOO, I CAN'T DO THIS.
YES YOU CAN BABY, JUST GET UP THERE AND SING!
BUT WHAT IF THEY DON'T LIKE ME?
THEY'RE GONNA LOVE YOU.
ORETTA LYNN & THE TRAILBLAZERS
AND THEY DID LOVE HER, SO MUCH THEY BOOKED HER FOR A WEEKLY GIG.
I CAN'T BELIEVE I GET PAID TO SING! I'M RICH!
LORETTA SAVED HER $5 PER GIG AND BOUGHT NEW PERFORMING CLOTHES.
BAR-K
DOO KEPT PULLING DOUBLE DUTY, WORKING HIS DAY JOB AND PROMOTING LORETTA ON THE SIDE. HE BOOKED HER ANYWHERE THERE WAS AN AUDIENCE. EVENTUALLY HE GOT HER A SPOT ON A TV TALENT SHOW,
AND THE WINNER IS... LORETTA LYNN!
WHERE SHE WON FIRST PRIZE!

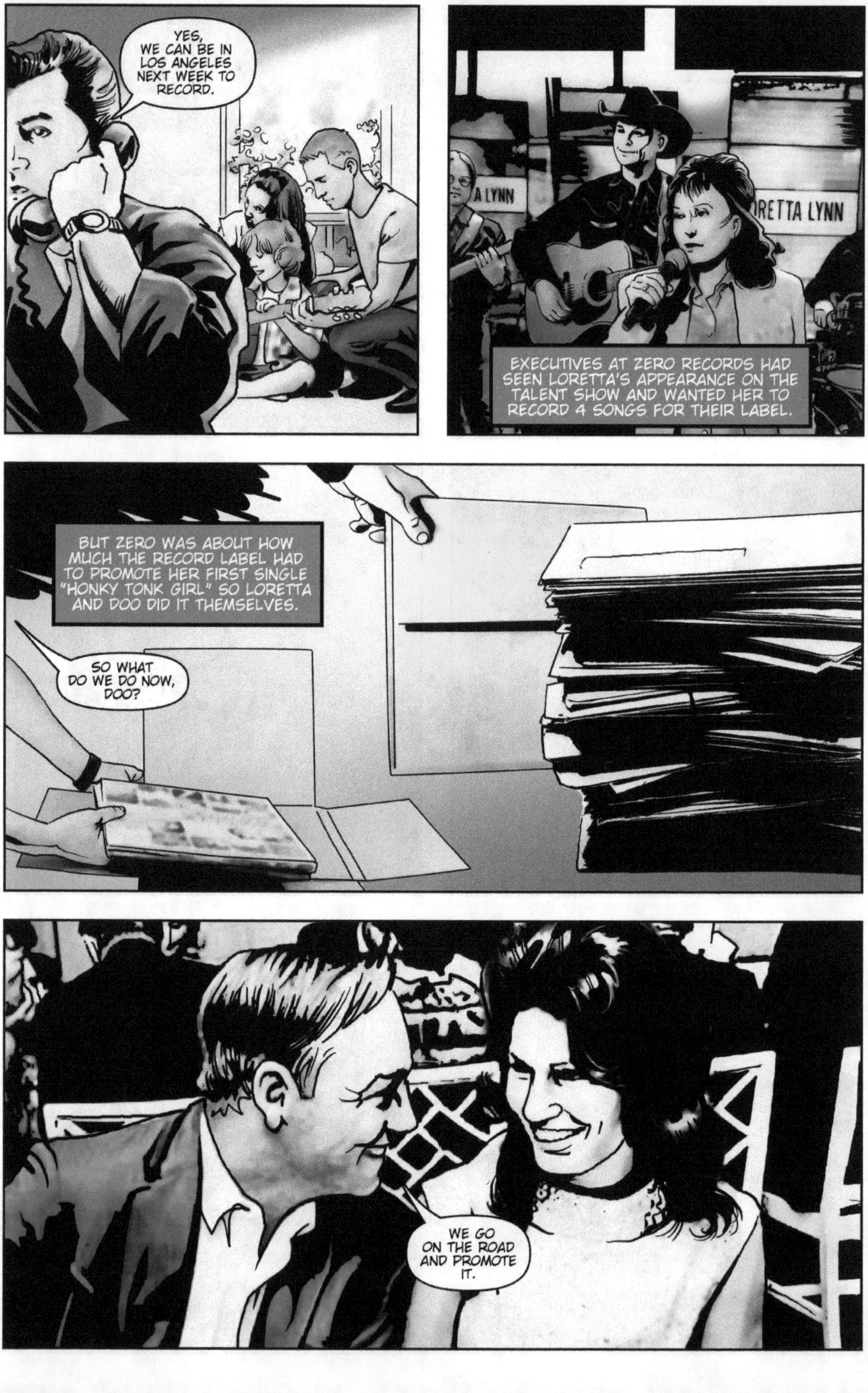
YES, WE CAN BE IN LOS ANGELES NEXT WEEK TO RECORD.
A LYNN
RETTA LYNN
EXECUTIVES AT ZERO RECORDS HAD SEEN LORETTA'S APPEARANCE ON THE TALENT SHOW AND WANTED HER TO RECORD 4 SONGS FOR THEIR LABEL.
BUT ZERO WAS ABOUT HOW MUCH THE RECORD LABEL HAD TO PROMOTE HER FIRST SINGLE "HONKY TONK GIRL" SO LORETTA AND DOO DID IT THEMSELVES.
SO WHAT DO WE DO NOW, DOO?
WE GO ON THE ROAD AND PROMOTE IT.

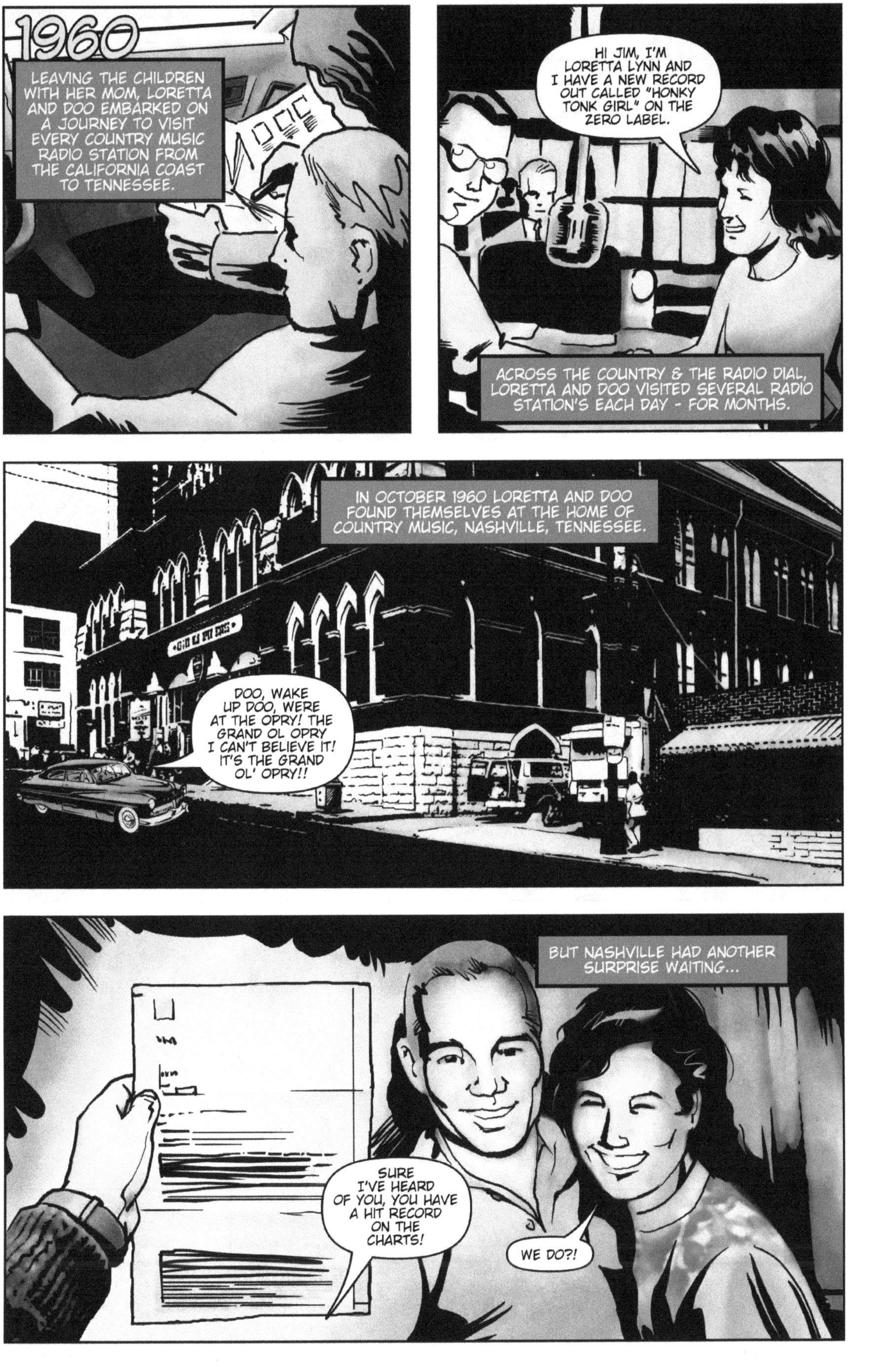
1960
LEAVING THE CHILDREN WITH HER MOM, LORETTA AND DOO EMBARKED ON A JOURNEY TO VISIT EVERY COUNTRY MUSIC RADIO STATION FROM THE CALIFORNIA COAST TO TENNESSEE.
HI JIM, I'M LORETTA LYNN AND I HAVE A NEW RECORD OUT CALLED "HONKY TONK GIRL" ON THE ZERO LABEL.
ACROSS THE COUNTRY & THE RADIO DIAL, LORETTA AND DOO VISITED SEVERAL RADIO STATION'S EACH DAY - FOR MONTHS.
IN OCTOBER 1960 LORETTA AND DOO FOUND THEMSELVES AT THE HOME OF COUNTRY MUSIC, NASHVILLE, TENNESSEE.
DOO, WAKE UP DOO, WERE AT THE OPRY! THE GRAND OL OPRY I CAN'T BELIEVE IT! IT'S THE GRAND OL' OPRY!!
BUT NASHVILLE HAD ANOTHER SURPRISE WAITING...
SURE I'VE HEARD OF YOU, YOU HAVE A HIT RECORD ON THE CHARTS!
WE DO?!

OCTOBER 15, 1960

LORETTA'S DREAM CAME TRUE, SHE PLAYED THE GRAND OL' OPRY FOR THE FIRST TIME.

AND AFTER THE COMMERCIAL BREAK ERNEST WILL INTRODUCE YOU, JUST WALK TO THE CENTER MIC.

AND NOW MAKING HER OPRY DEBUT, ONE OF THE NEWEST GIRL SINGERS IN THE BUSINESS, LORETTA LYNN!

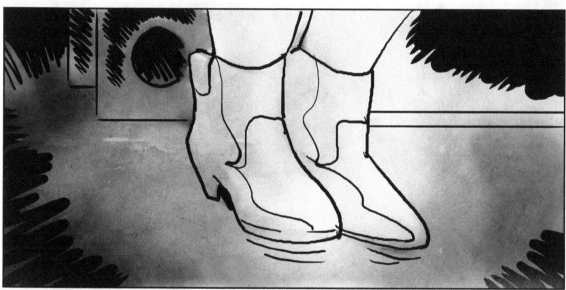

I DID IT! I DID IT!! OH DAGNABIT...

WHAT?

I FORGOT TO LISTEN TO MYSELF SING.

TWO YEARS LATER THE OPRY INVITED LORETTA TO BECOME A MEMBER.

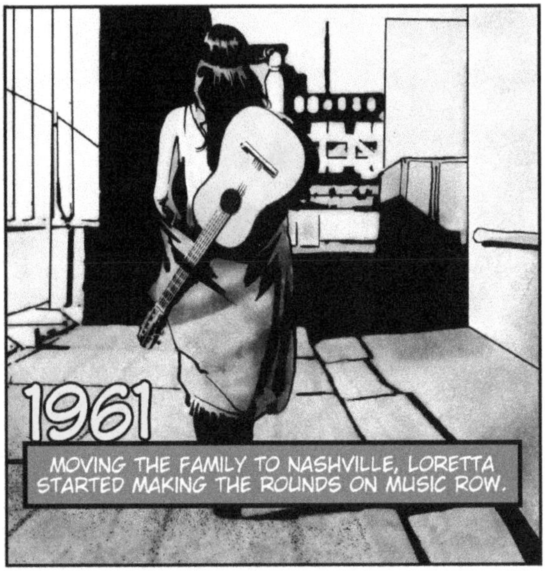
1961
MOVING THE FAMILY TO NASHVILLE, LORETTA STARTED MAKING THE ROUNDS ON MUSIC ROW.

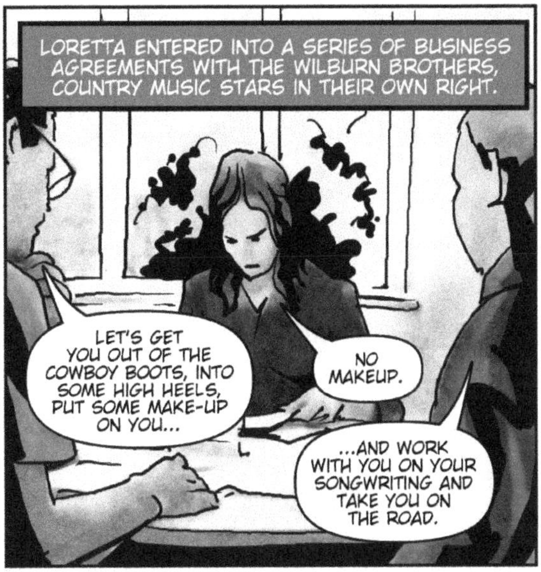
LORETTA ENTERED INTO A SERIES OF BUSINESS AGREEMENTS WITH THE WILBURN BROTHERS, COUNTRY MUSIC STARS IN THEIR OWN RIGHT.
LET'S GET YOU OUT OF THE COWBOY BOOTS, INTO SOME HIGH HEELS, PUT SOME MAKE-UP ON YOU...
NO MAKEUP.
...AND WORK WITH YOU ON YOUR SONGWRITING AND TAKE YOU ON THE ROAD.

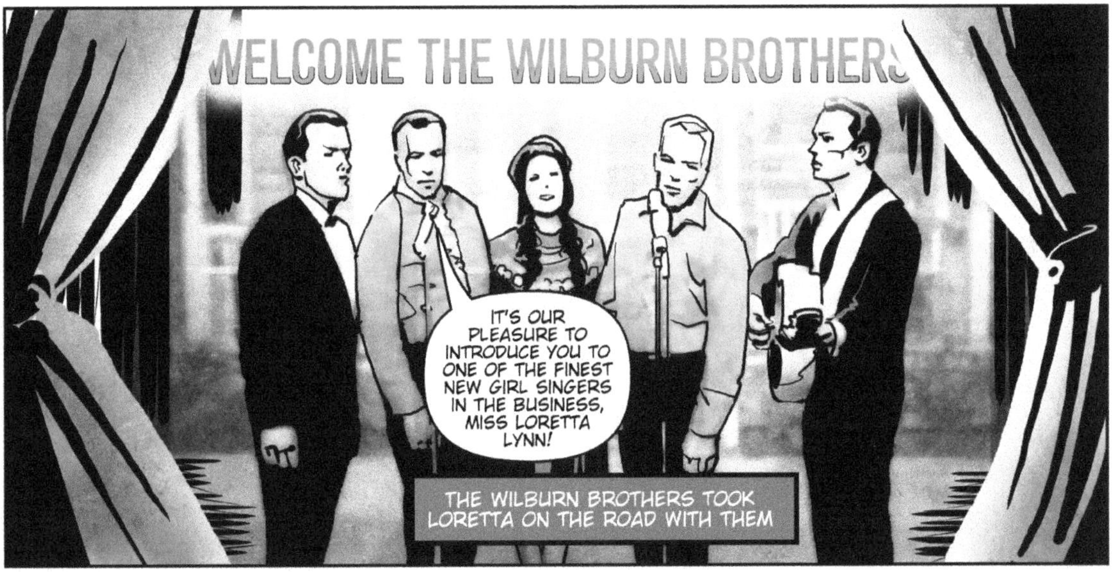
WELCOME THE WILBURN BROTHERS
IT'S OUR PLEASURE TO INTRODUCE YOU TO ONE OF THE FINEST NEW GIRL SINGERS IN THE BUSINESS, MISS LORETTA LYNN!
THE WILBURN BROTHERS TOOK LORETTA ON THE ROAD WITH THEM

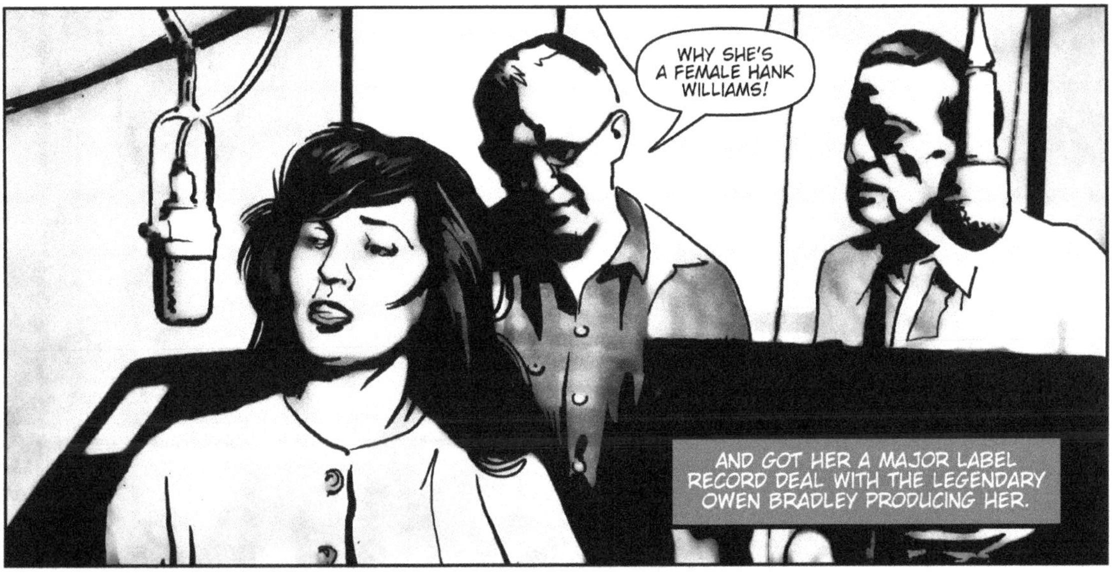
WHY SHE'S A FEMALE HANK WILLIAMS!
AND GOT HER A MAJOR LABEL RECORD DEAL WITH THE LEGENDARY OWEN BRADLEY PRODUCING HER.

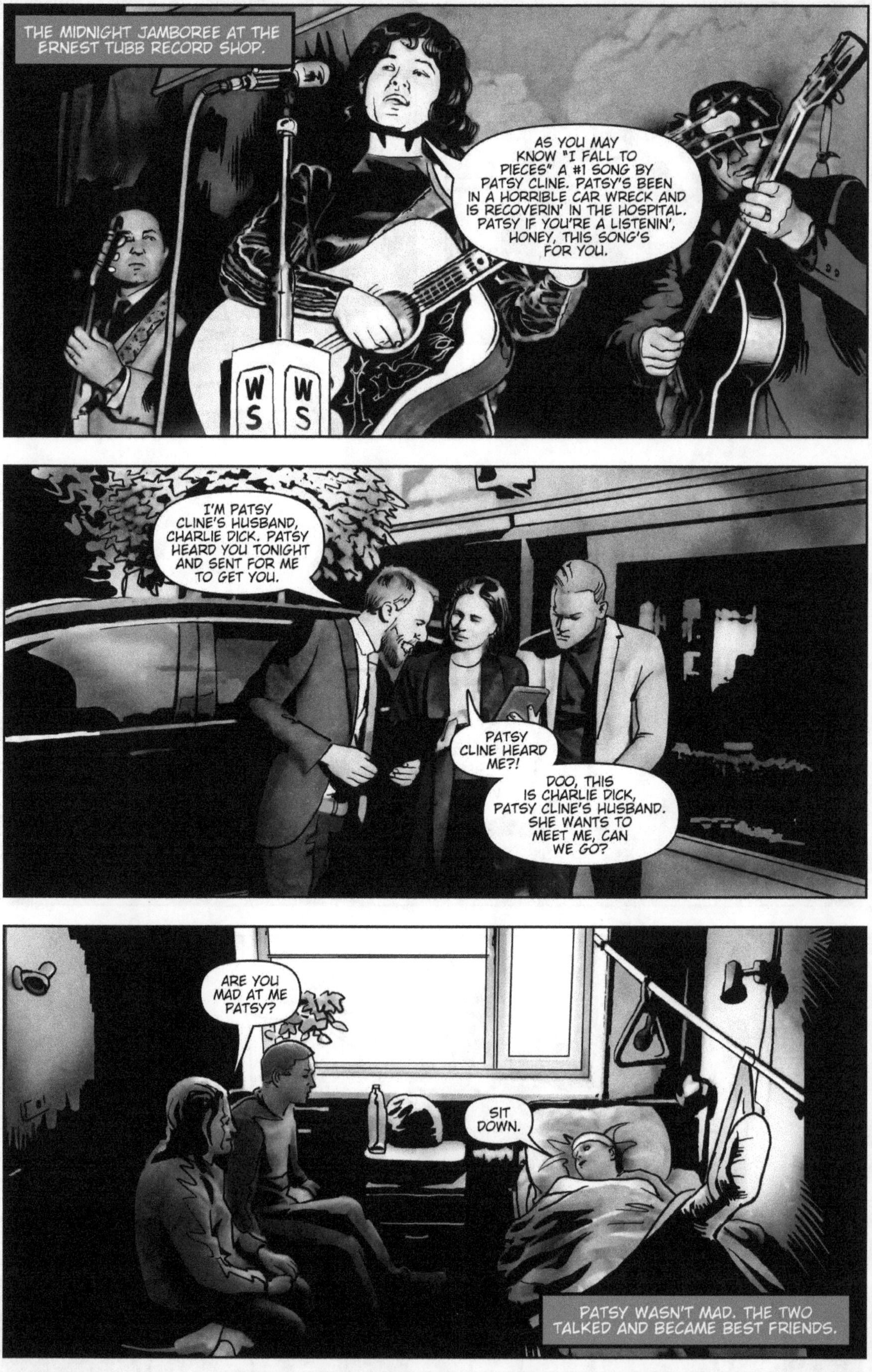
THE MIDNIGHT JAMBOREE AT THE ERNEST TUBB RECORD SHOP.
AS YOU MAY KNOW "I FALL TO PIECES" A #1 SONG BY PATSY CLINE. PATSY'S BEEN IN A HORRIBLE CAR WRECK AND IS RECOVERIN' IN THE HOSPITAL. PATSY IF YOU'RE A LISTENIN', HONEY, THIS SONG'S FOR YOU.
W S
W S
I'M PATSY CLINE'S HUSBAND, CHARLIE DICK. PATSY HEARD YOU TONIGHT AND SENT FOR ME TO GET YOU.
PATSY CLINE HEARD ME?!
DOO, THIS IS CHARLIE DICK, PATSY CLINE'S HUSBAND. SHE WANTS TO MEET ME, CAN WE GO?
ARE YOU MAD AT ME PATSY?
SIT DOWN.
PATSY WASN'T MAD. THE TWO TALKED AND BECAME BEST FRIENDS.

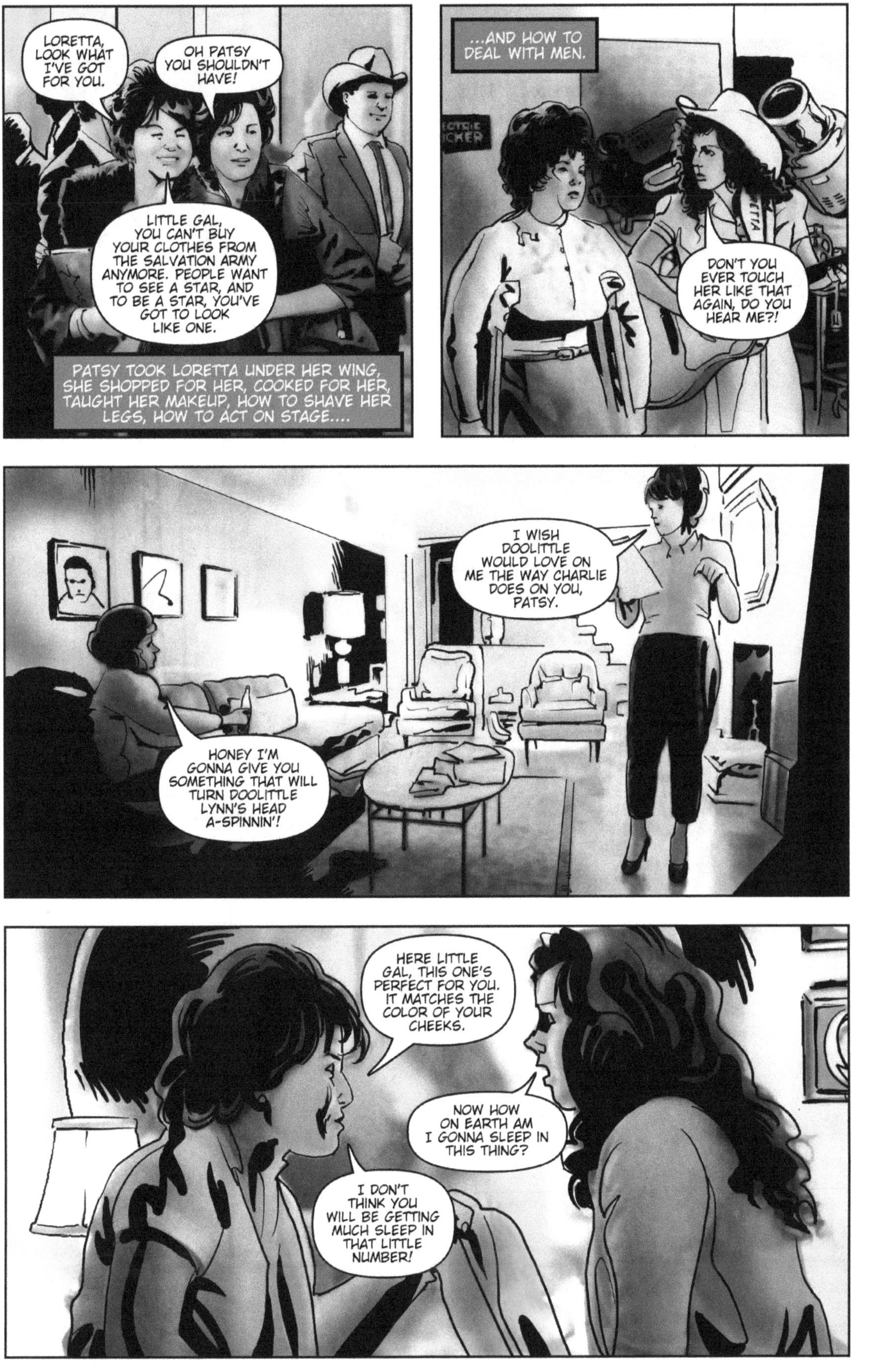
LORETTA, LOOK WHAT I'VE GOT FOR YOU.
OH PATSY YOU SHOULDN'T HAVE!
LITTLE GAL, YOU CAN'T BUY YOUR CLOTHES FROM THE SALVATION ARMY ANYMORE. PEOPLE WANT TO SEE A STAR, AND TO BE A STAR, YOU'VE GOT TO LOOK LIKE ONE.
PATSY TOOK LORETTA UNDER HER WING, SHE SHOPPED FOR HER, COOKED FOR HER, TAUGHT HER MAKEUP, HOW TO SHAVE HER LEGS, HOW TO ACT ON STAGE....
...AND HOW TO DEAL WITH MEN.
DON'T YOU EVER TOUCH HER LIKE THAT AGAIN, DO YOU HEAR ME?!
I WISH DOOLITTLE WOULD LOVE ON ME THE WAY CHARLIE DOES ON YOU, PATSY.
HONEY I'M GONNA GIVE YOU SOMETHING THAT WILL TURN DOOLITTLE LYNN'S HEAD A-SPINNIN'!
HERE LITTLE GAL, THIS ONE'S PERFECT FOR YOU. IT MATCHES THE COLOR OF YOUR CHEEKS.
NOW HOW ON EARTH AM I GONNA SLEEP IN THIS THING?
I DON'T THINK YOU WILL BE GETTING MUCH SLEEP IN THAT LITTLE NUMBER!

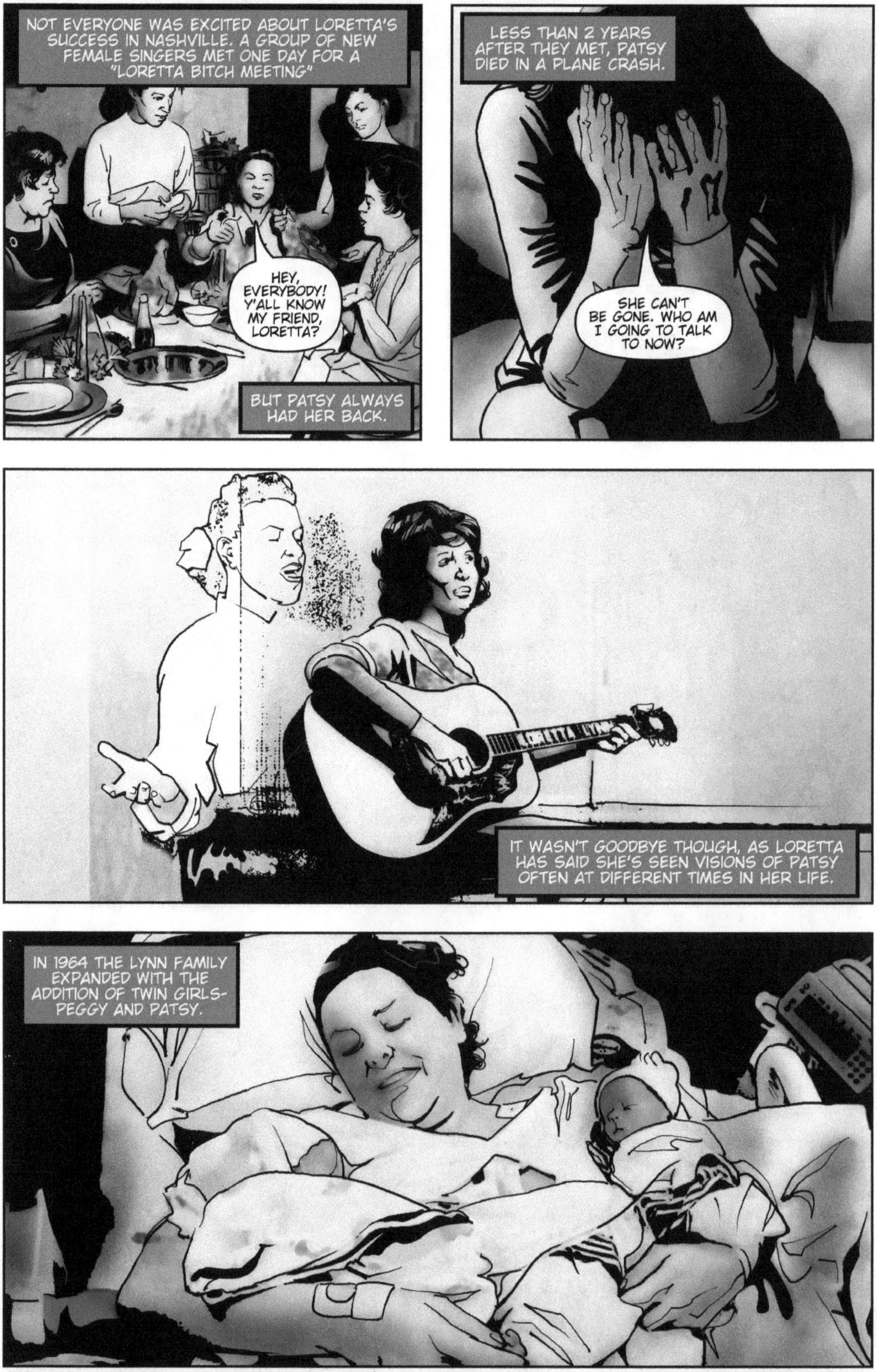
NOT EVERYONE WAS EXCITED ABOUT LORETTA'S SUCCESS IN NASHVILLE. A GROUP OF NEW FEMALE SINGERS MET ONE DAY FOR A "LORETTA BITCH MEETING"
HEY, EVERYBODY! Y'ALL KNOW MY FRIEND, LORETTA?
BUT PATSY ALWAYS HAD HER BACK.
LESS THAN 2 YEARS AFTER THEY MET, PATSY DIED IN A PLANE CRASH.
SHE CAN'T BE GONE. WHO AM I GOING TO TALK TO NOW?
IT WASN'T GOODBYE THOUGH, AS LORETTA HAS SAID SHE'S SEEN VISIONS OF PATSY OFTEN AT DIFFERENT TIMES IN HER LIFE.
IN 1964 THE LYNN FAMILY EXPANDED WITH THE ADDITION OF TWIN GIRLS- PEGGY AND PATSY.

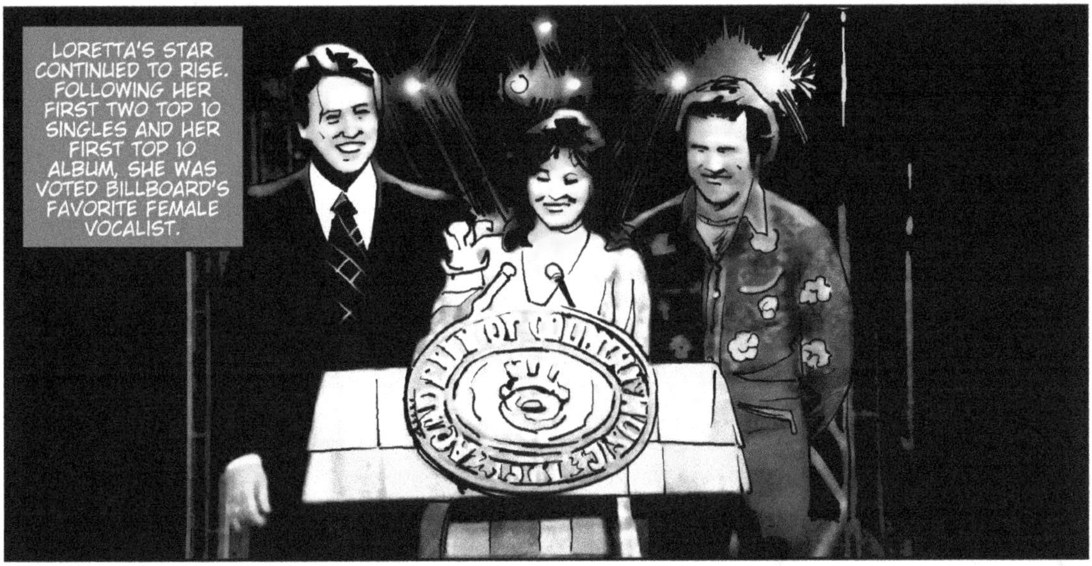
LORETTA'S STAR CONTINUED TO RISE. FOLLOWING HER FIRST TWO TOP 10 SINGLES AND HER FIRST TOP 10 ALBUM, SHE WAS VOTED BILLBOARD'S FAVORITE FEMALE VOCALIST.

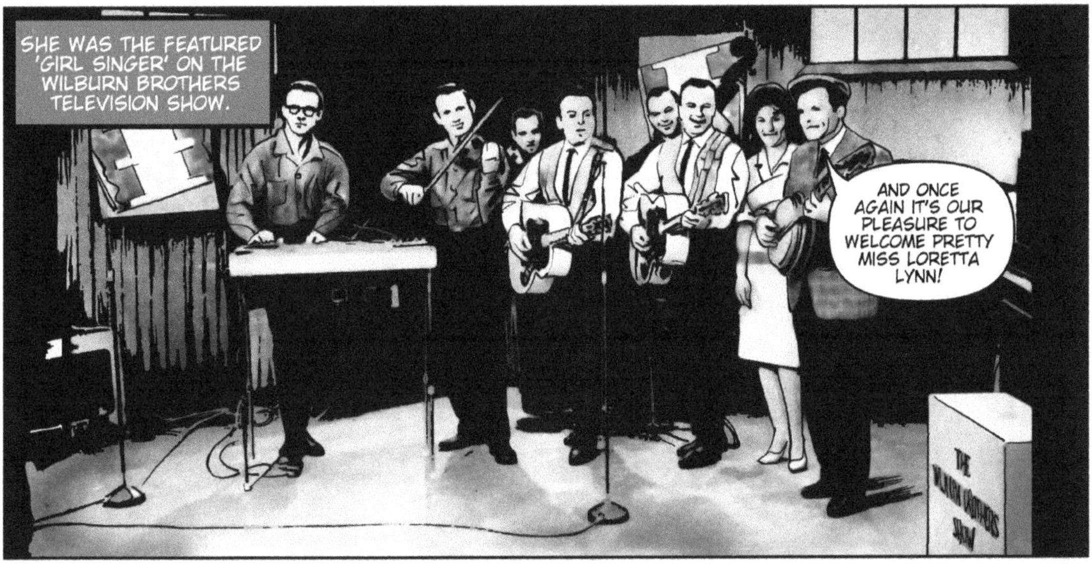
SHE WAS THE FEATURED 'GIRL SINGER' ON THE WILBURN BROTHERS TELEVISION SHOW.
AND ONCE AGAIN IT'S OUR PLEASURE TO WELCOME PRETTY MISS LORETTA LYNN!

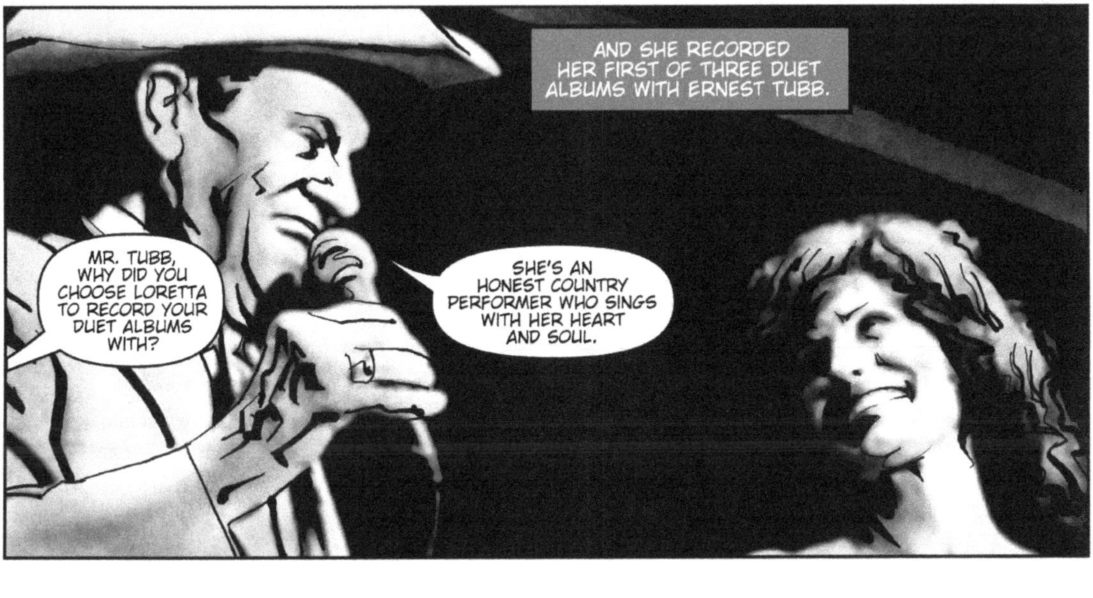
AND SHE RECORDED HER FIRST OF THREE DUET ALBUMS WITH ERNEST TUBB.
MR. TUBB, WHY DID YOU CHOOSE LORETTA TO RECORD YOUR DUET ALBUMS WITH?
SHE'S AN HONEST COUNTRY PERFORMER WHO SINGS WITH HER HEART AND SOUL.

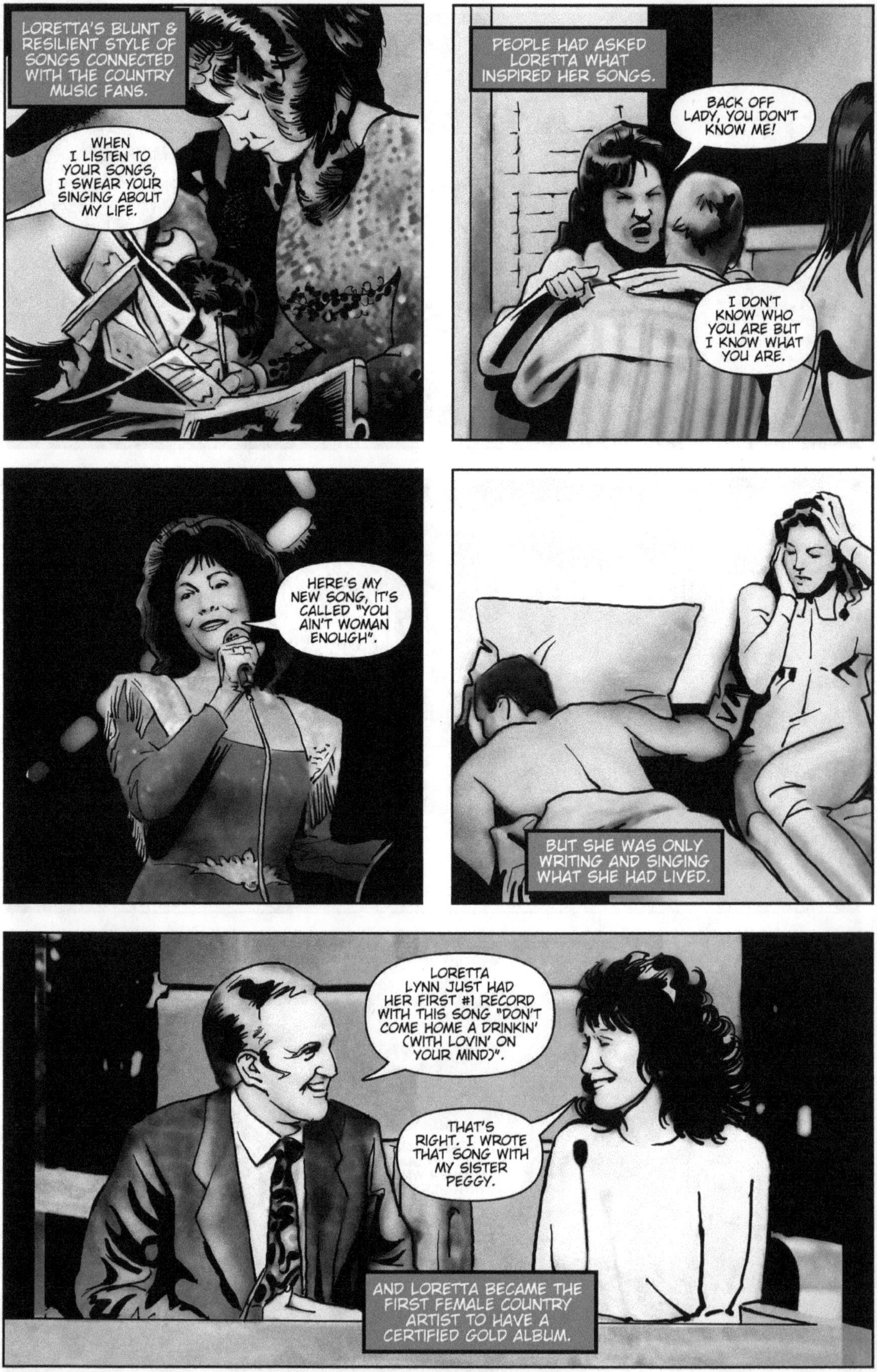
LORETTA'S BLUNT & RESILIENT STYLE OF SONGS CONNECTED WITH THE COUNTRY MUSIC FANS.
WHEN I LISTEN TO YOUR SONGS, I SWEAR YOUR SINGING ABOUT MY LIFE.
PEOPLE HAD ASKED LORETTA WHAT INSPIRED HER SONGS.
BACK OFF LADY, YOU DON'T KNOW ME!
I DON'T KNOW WHO YOU ARE BUT I KNOW WHAT YOU ARE.
HERE'S MY NEW SONG, IT'S CALLED "YOU AIN'T WOMAN ENOUGH".
BUT SHE WAS ONLY WRITING AND SINGING WHAT SHE HAD LIVED.
LORETTA LYNN JUST HAD HER FIRST #1 RECORD WITH THIS SONG "DON'T COME HOME A DRINKIN' (WITH LOVIN' ON YOUR MIND)".
THAT'S RIGHT. I WROTE THAT SONG WITH MY SISTER PEGGY.
AND LORETTA BECAME THE FIRST FEMALE COUNTRY ARTIST TO HAVE A CERTIFIED GOLD ALBUM.

COUNTRY MUSIC WASN'T USED TO HAVING FEMALE SINGERS SINGING ABOUT SUBJECTS LIKE LORETTA DID. 14 OF HER SONGS WOULD END UP GETTING BANNED.

BUT THAT DIDN'T STOP THEM FROM BECOMING HIT RECORDS...

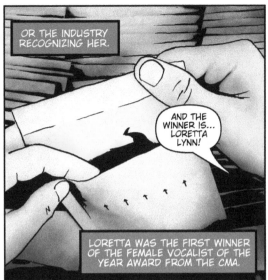

OR THE INDUSTRY RECOGNIZING HER.

AND THE WINNER IS... LORETTA LYNN!

LORETTA WAS THE FIRST WINNER OF THE FEMALE VOCALIST OF THE YEAR AWARD FROM THE CMA.

1969

BUT IT WAS THE MOST AUTOBIOGRAPHICAL SONG SHE EVER WROTE THAT FANS TOOK TO THE MOST,

AND BECAME HER SIGNATURE SONG.

THAT SONG TOOK HER FROM BEING A COAL MINER'S DAUGHTER TO BEING THE COAL MINER'S DAUGHTER,

LOOK! IT'S THE COAL MINER'S DAUGHTER!

AND SHE WENT FROM BEING A STAR TO A SUPERSTAR!

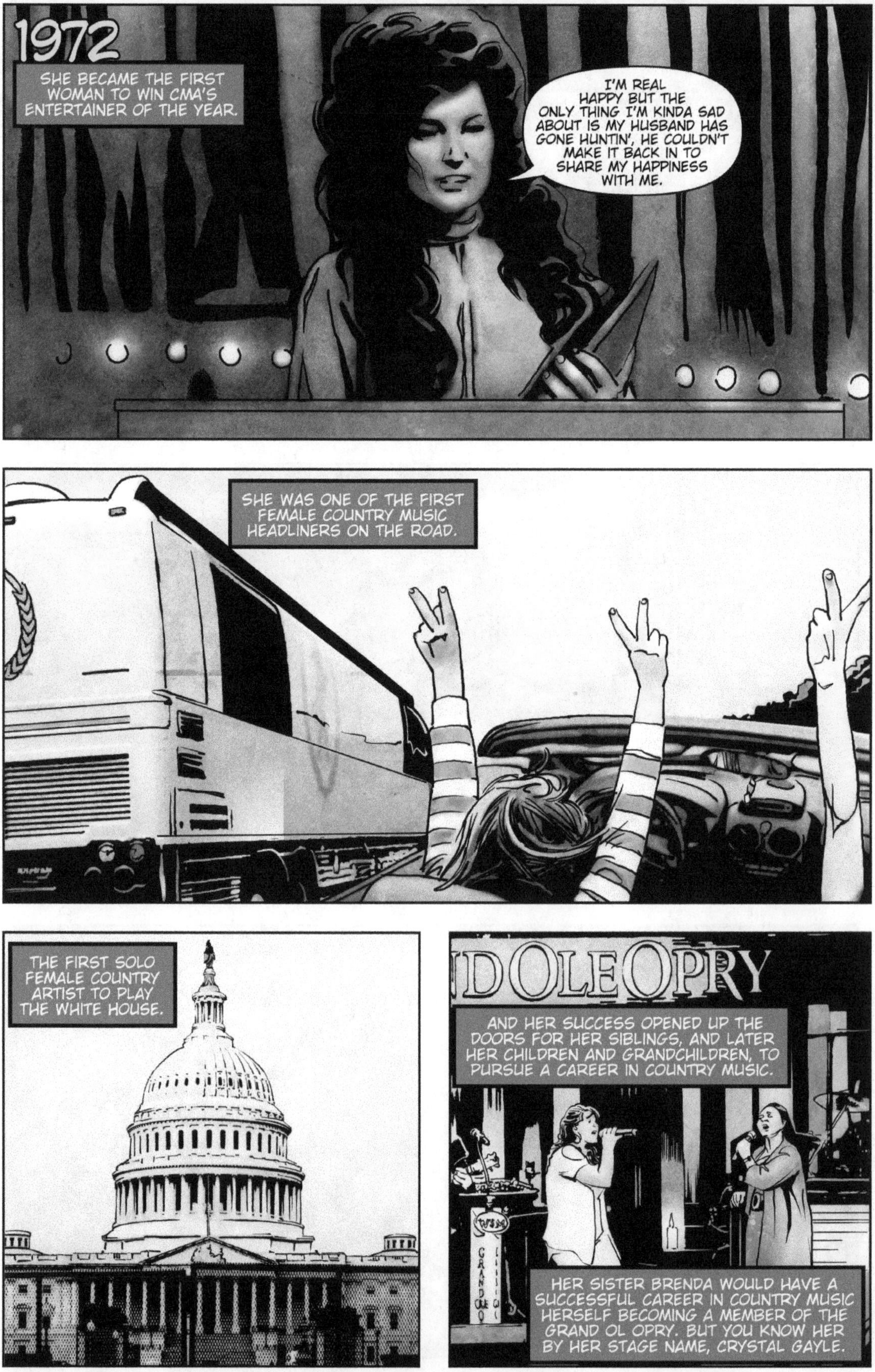
1972
SHE BECAME THE FIRST WOMAN TO WIN CMA'S ENTERTAINER OF THE YEAR.
I'M REAL HAPPY BUT THE ONLY THING I'M KINDA SAD ABOUT IS MY HUSBAND HAS GONE HUNTIN', HE COULDN'T MAKE IT BACK IN TO SHARE MY HAPPINESS WITH ME.
SHE WAS ONE OF THE FIRST FEMALE COUNTRY MUSIC HEADLINERS ON THE ROAD.
THE FIRST SOLO FEMALE COUNTRY ARTIST TO PLAY THE WHITE HOUSE.
AND HER SUCCESS OPENED UP THE DOORS FOR HER SIBLINGS, AND LATER HER CHILDREN AND GRANDCHILDREN, TO PURSUE A CAREER IN COUNTRY MUSIC.
HER SISTER BRENDA WOULD HAVE A SUCCESSFUL CAREER IN COUNTRY MUSIC HERSELF BECOMING A MEMBER OF THE GRAND OL OPRY. BUT YOU KNOW HER BY HER STAGE NAME, CRYSTAL GAYLE.

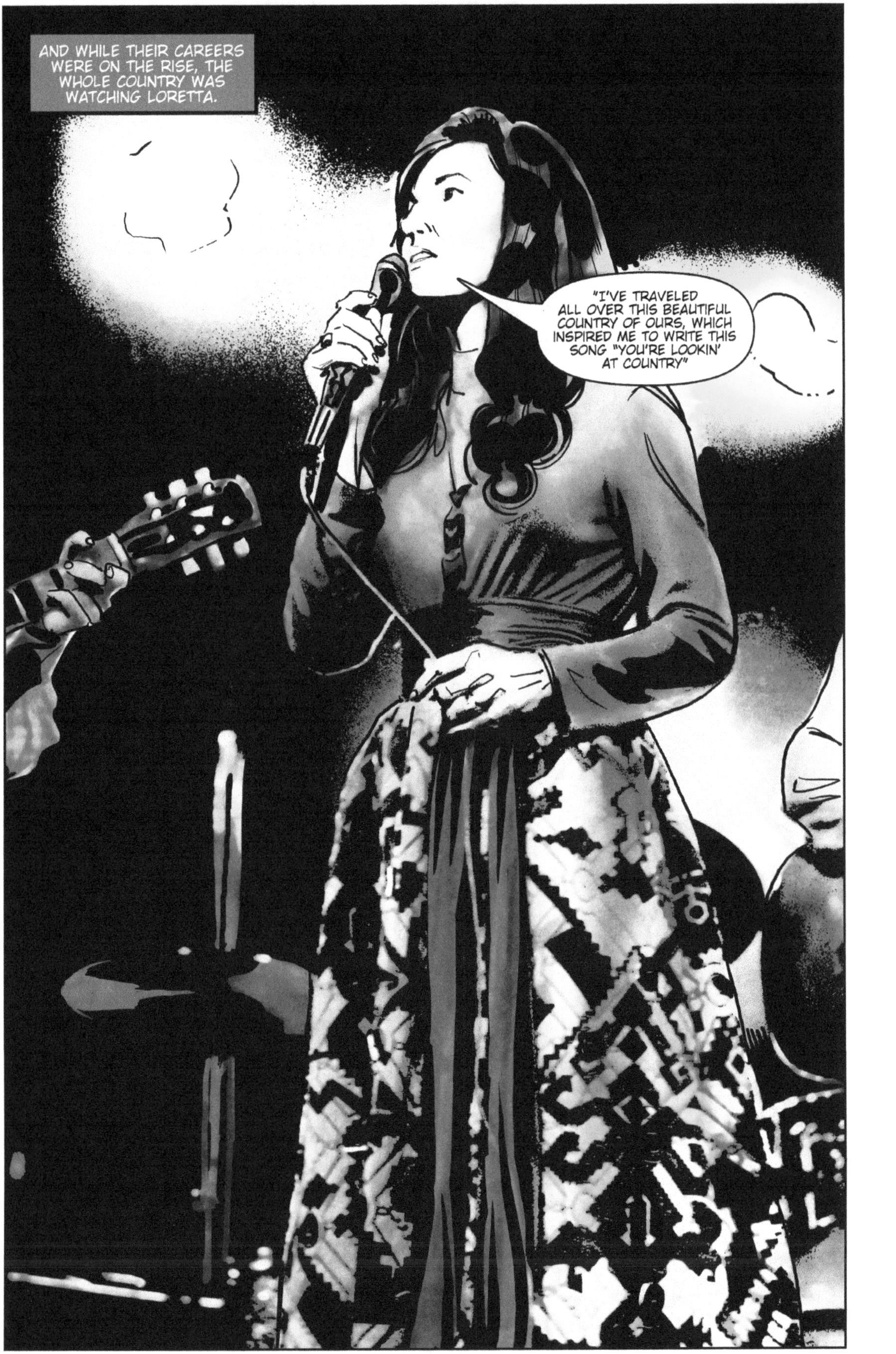
AND WHILE THEIR CAREERS WERE ON THE RISE, THE WHOLE COUNTRY WAS WATCHING LORETTA.
"I'VE TRAVELED ALL OVER THIS BEAUTIFUL COUNTRY OF OURS, WHICH INSPIRED ME TO WRITE THIS SONG "YOU'RE LOOKIN' AT COUNTRY"

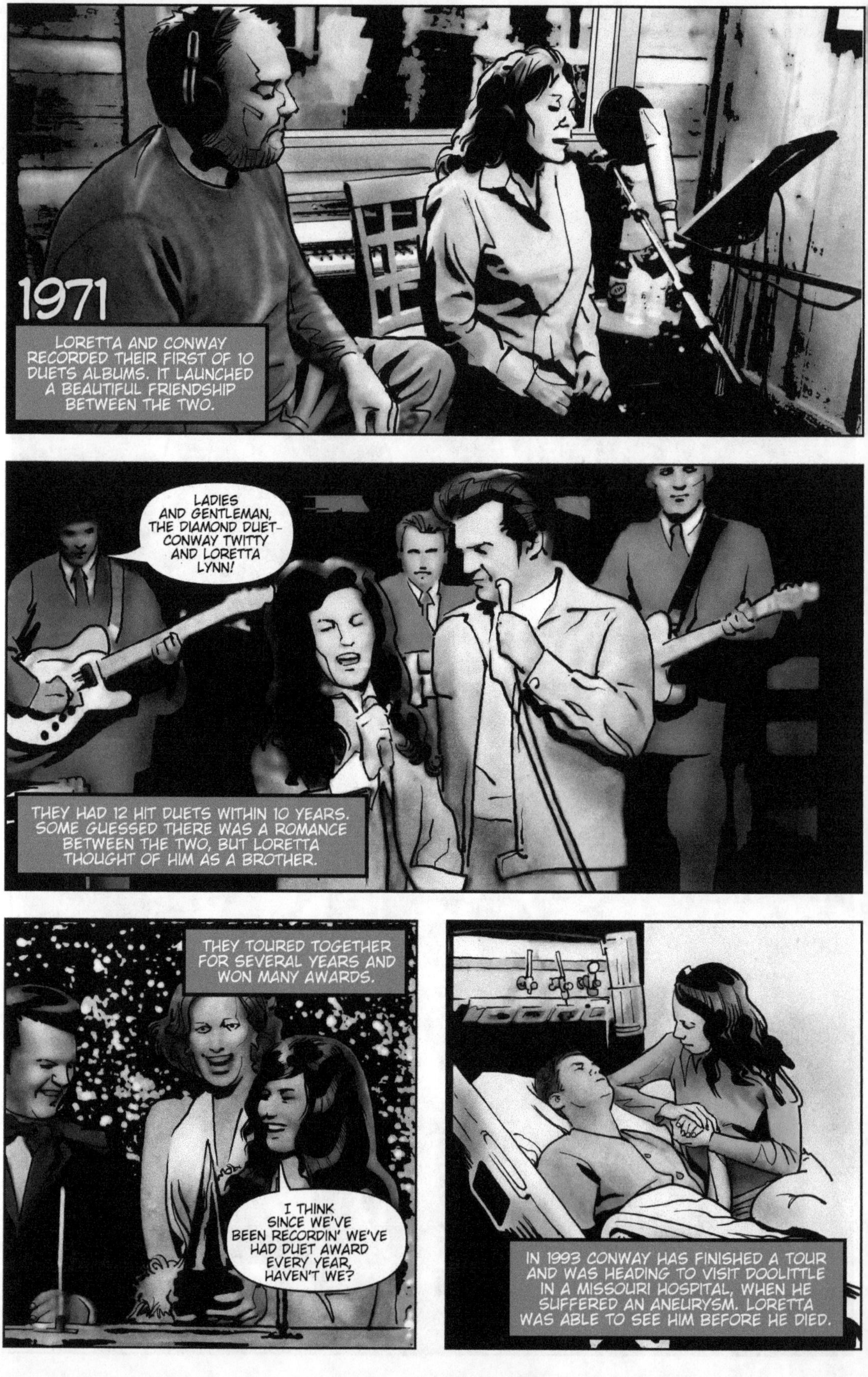
1971
LORETTA AND CONWAY RECORDED THEIR FIRST OF 10 DUETS ALBUMS. IT LAUNCHED A BEAUTIFUL FRIENDSHIP BETWEEN THE TWO.
LADIES AND GENTLEMAN, THE DIAMOND DUET- CONWAY TWITTY AND LORETTA LYNN!
THEY HAD 12 HIT DUETS WITHIN 10 YEARS. SOME GUESSED THERE WAS A ROMANCE BETWEEN THE TWO, BUT LORETTA THOUGHT OF HIM AS A BROTHER.
THEY TOURED TOGETHER FOR SEVERAL YEARS AND WON MANY AWARDS.
I THINK SINCE WE'VE BEEN RECORDIN' WE'VE HAD DUET AWARD EVERY YEAR, HAVEN'T WE?
IN 1993 CONWAY HAS FINISHED A TOUR AND WAS HEADING TO VISIT DOOLITTLE IN A MISSOURI HOSPITAL, WHEN HE SUFFERED AN ANEURYSM. LORETTA WAS ABLE TO SEE HIM BEFORE HE DIED.

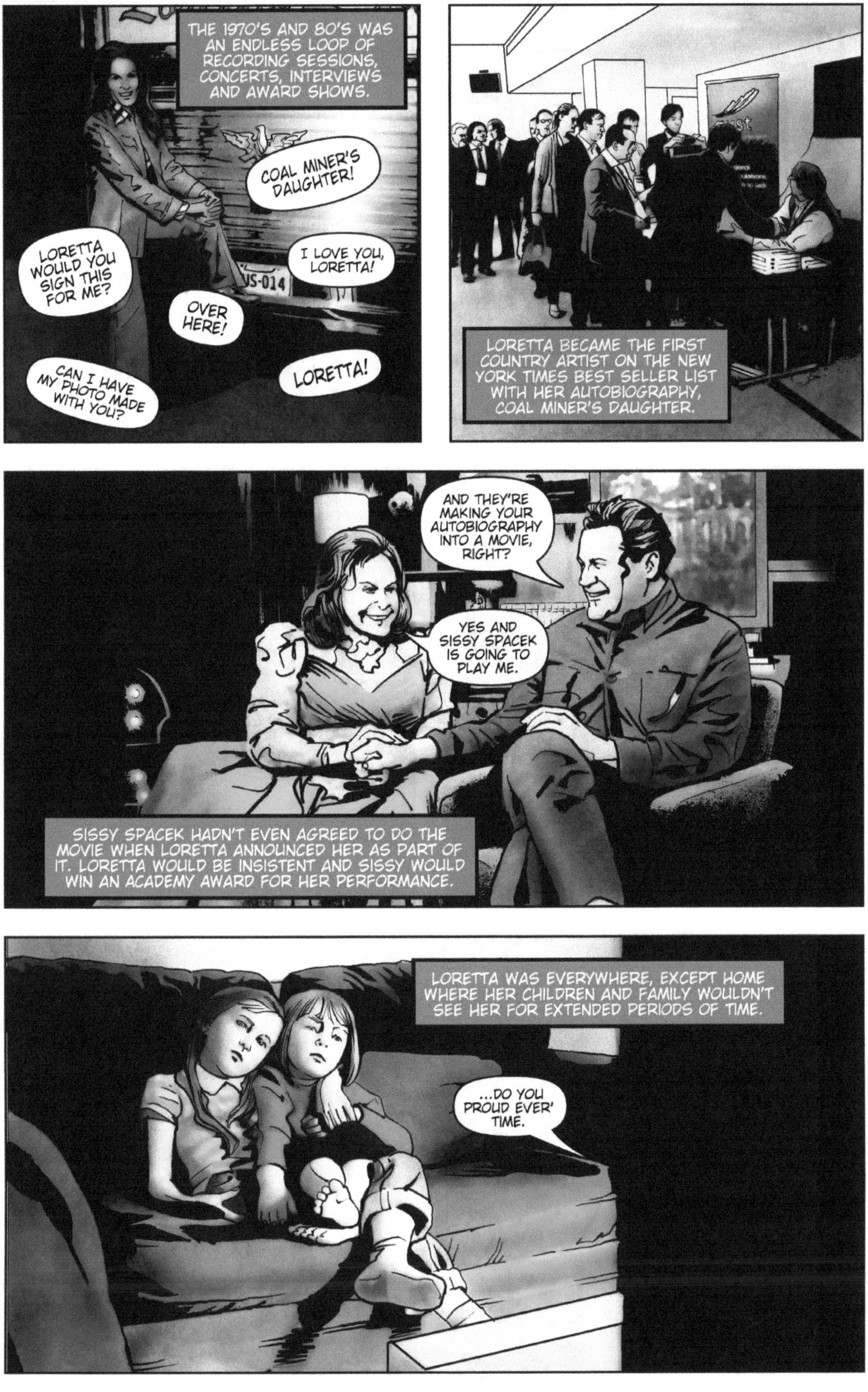
THE 1970'S AND 80'S WAS AN ENDLESS LOOP OF RECORDING SESSIONS, CONCERTS, INTERVIEWS AND AWARD SHOWS.
COAL MINER'S DAUGHTER!
LORETTA WOULD YOU SIGN THIS FOR ME?
I LOVE YOU, LORETTA!
OVER HERE!
CAN I HAVE MY PHOTO MADE WITH YOU?
LORETTA!
LORETTA BECAME THE FIRST COUNTRY ARTIST ON THE NEW YORK TIMES BEST SELLER LIST WITH HER AUTOBIOGRAPHY, COAL MINER'S DAUGHTER.
AND THEY'RE MAKING YOUR AUTOBIOGRAPHY INTO A MOVIE, RIGHT?
YES AND SISSY SPACEK IS GOING TO PLAY ME.
SISSY SPACEK HADN'T EVEN AGREED TO DO THE MOVIE WHEN LORETTA ANNOUNCED HER AS PART OF IT. LORETTA WOULD BE INSISTENT AND SISSY WOULD WIN AN ACADEMY AWARD FOR HER PERFORMANCE.
LORETTA WAS EVERYWHERE, EXCEPT HOME WHERE HER CHILDREN AND FAMILY WOULDN'T SEE HER FOR EXTENDED PERIODS OF TIME.
...DO YOU PROUD EVER' TIME.

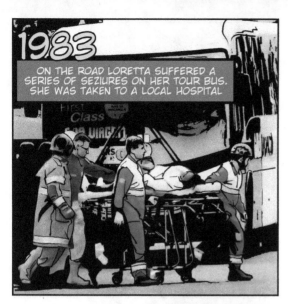

1983
ON THE ROAD LORETTA SUFFERED A SERIES OF SEIZURES ON HER TOUR BUS. SHE WAS TAKEN TO A LOCAL HOSPITAL

LORETTA'S SON JACK BENNY LYNN HAD DIED FROM DROWNING AT THE AGE OF 34.

WE'VE LOST OUR BOY.

HIS TIME OF DEATH COINCIDED WITH HER SEIZURES ON THE BUS.

ON SPEAKING ABOUT JACK BENNY'S DEATH, LORETTA WOULD SAY "MY LIFE HAS RUN FROM MISERY TO HAPPINESS AND SOMETIMES BACK TO MISERY".

THIS AIN'T HAPPENIN' TO ME, GETTIN' IN THE HALL OF FAME, I CAN SEE THE HALL OF SHAME BUT NOT THE HALL OF FAME.

THE ACCOLADES CONTINUED TO POUR IN FOR LORETTA. SHE WAS THE ARTIST OF THE DECADE FOR THE 1970'S FROM THE ACADEMY OF COUNTRY MUSIC, SHE WAS NAMED THE LIVING LEGEND BY MUSIC CITY NEWS IN 1986 AND IN 1988 EARNED THE HIGHEST HONOR IN COUNTRY MUSIC - ELECTION TO THE COUNTRY MUSIC HALL OF FAME.

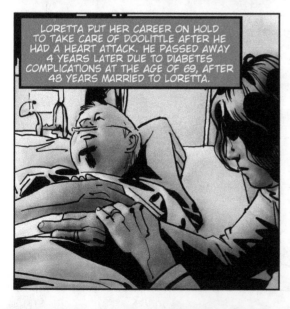

LORETTA PUT HER CAREER ON HOLD TO TAKE CARE OF DOOLITTLE AFTER HE HAD A HEART ATTACK. HE PASSED AWAY 4 YEARS LATER DUE TO DIABETES COMPLICATIONS AT THE AGE OF 69, AFTER 48 YEARS MARRIED TO LORETTA.

LORETTA WOULD SAY "OF COURSE YOU NEVER GET OVER LOSIN' PEOPLE LIKE THAT. YOU JUST LEARN TO LIVE WITH IT. BUT I THINK IT HELPS IF YOU STAY BUSY"

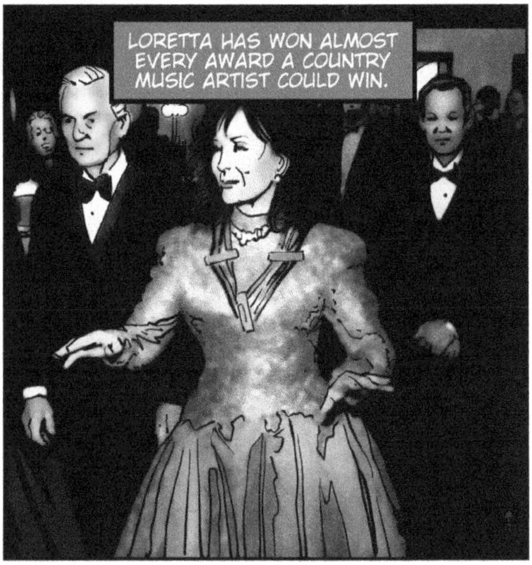
LORETTA HAS WON ALMOST EVERY AWARD A COUNTRY MUSIC ARTIST COULD WIN.

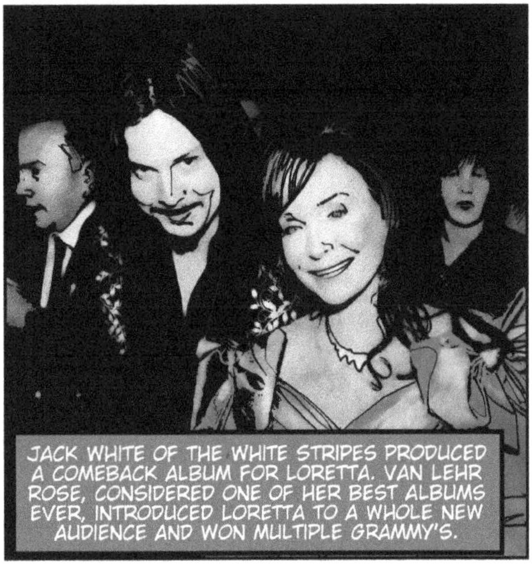
JACK WHITE OF THE WHITE STRIPES PRODUCED A COMEBACK ALBUM FOR LORETTA. VAN LEHR ROSE, CONSIDERED ONE OF HER BEST ALBUMS EVER, INTRODUCED LORETTA TO A WHOLE NEW AUDIENCE AND WON MULTIPLE GRAMMY'S.

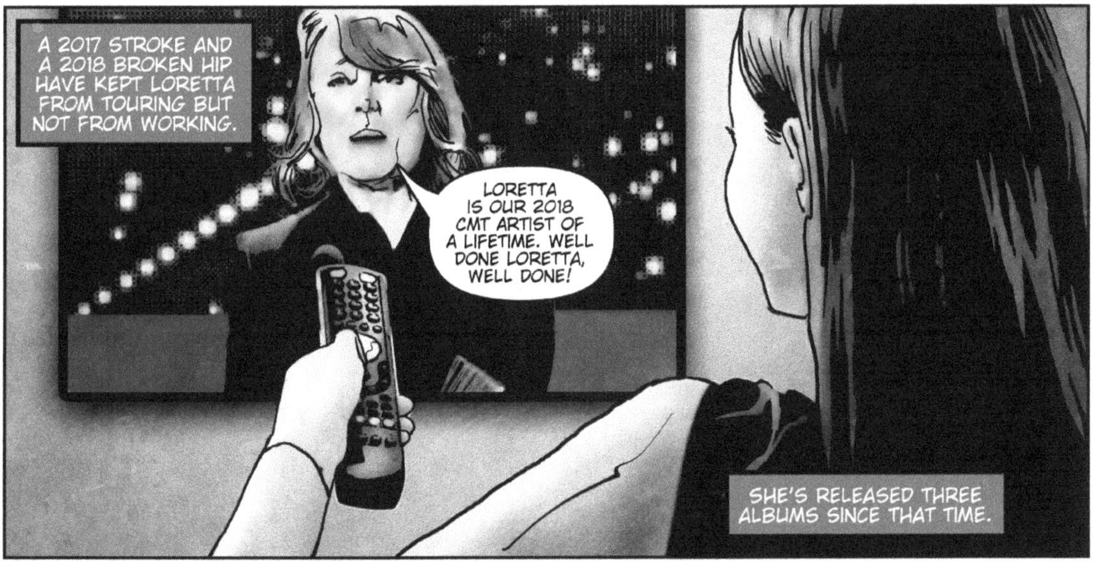
A 2017 STROKE AND A 2018 BROKEN HIP HAVE KEPT LORETTA FROM TOURING BUT NOT FROM WORKING.
LORETTA IS OUR 2018 CMT ARTIST OF A LIFETIME. WELL DONE LORETTA, WELL DONE!
SHE'S RELEASED THREE ALBUMS SINCE THAT TIME.

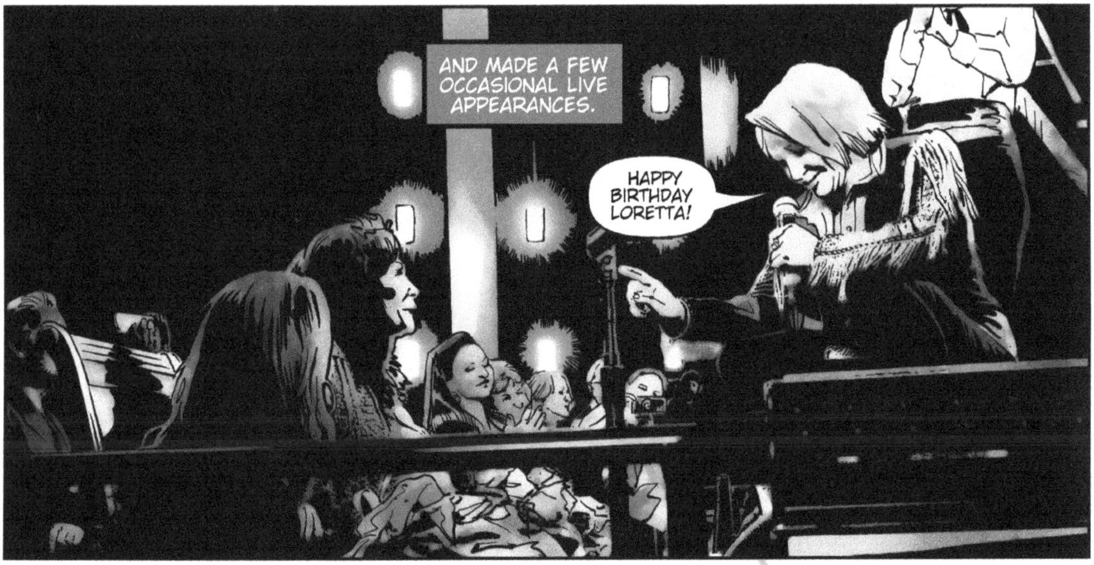
AND MADE A FEW OCCASIONAL LIVE APPEARANCES.
HAPPY BIRTHDAY LORETTA!

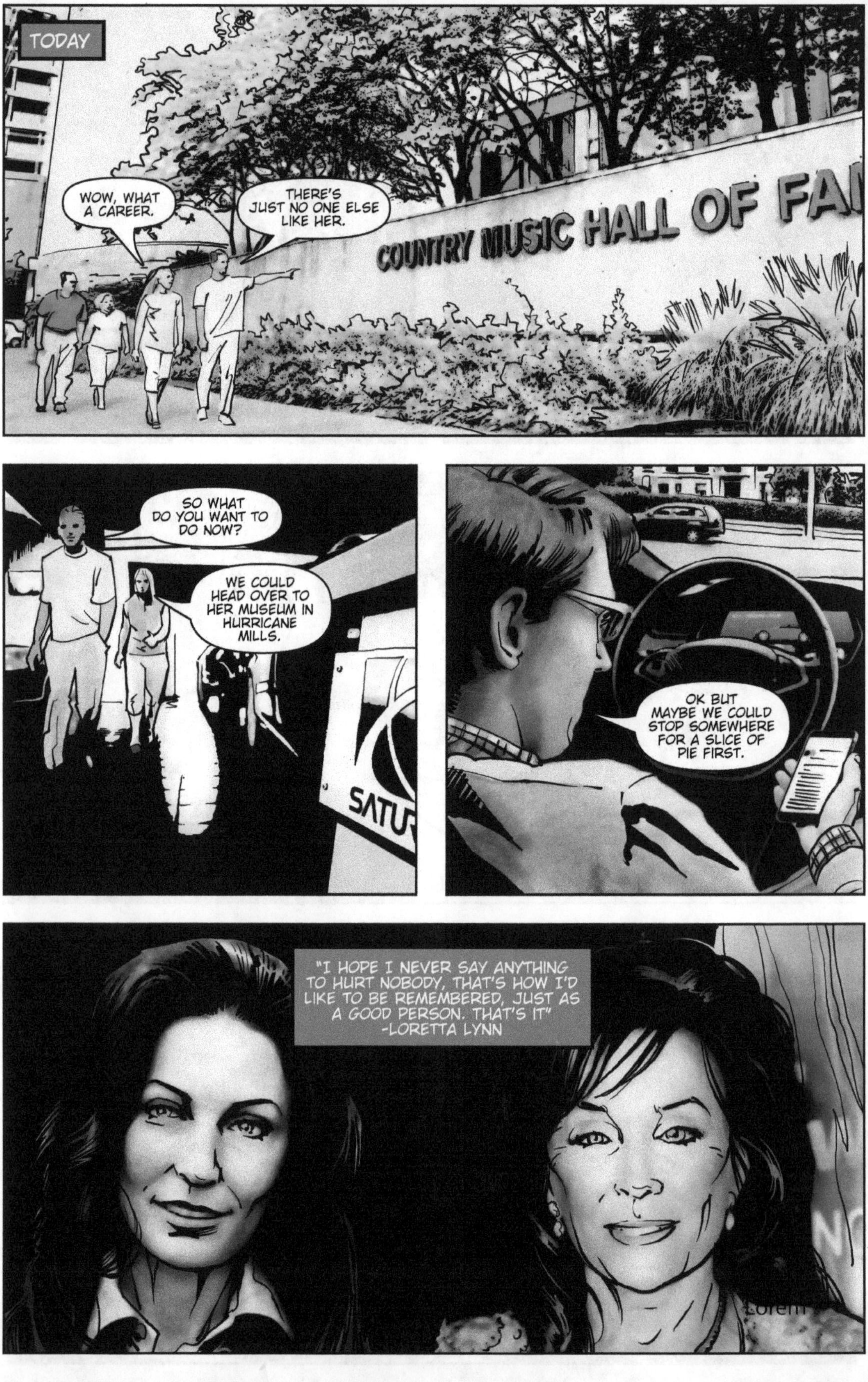
TODAY
WOW, WHAT A CAREER.
THERE'S JUST NO ONE ELSE LIKE HER.
COUNTRY MUSIC HALL OF
SO WHAT DO YOU WANT TO DO NOW?
WE COULD HEAD OVER TO HER MUSEUM IN HURRICANE MILLS.
OK BUT MAYBE WE COULD STOP SOMEWHERE FOR A SLICE OF PIE FIRST.
"I HOPE I NEVER SAY ANYTHING TO HURT NOBODY, THAT'S HOW I'D LIKE TO BE REMEMBERED, JUST AS A GOOD PERSON. THAT'S IT"
-LORETTA LYNN

TIDALWAVE COMICS

Ryan McCall — Writer

Martin Gimenez — Art

Benjamin Glibert — Letters

Darren G. Davis — Editor

Pablo Martinena — Cover

Cover B: Ramon Salas

Special thanks to Douglass Mabry & Aaron Smith

Darren G. Davis
Publisher

Maggie Jessup
Publicity

Susan Ferris
Entertainment Manager

Steven Diggs Jr.
Marketing Manager

TIDALWAVE PRODUCTIONS

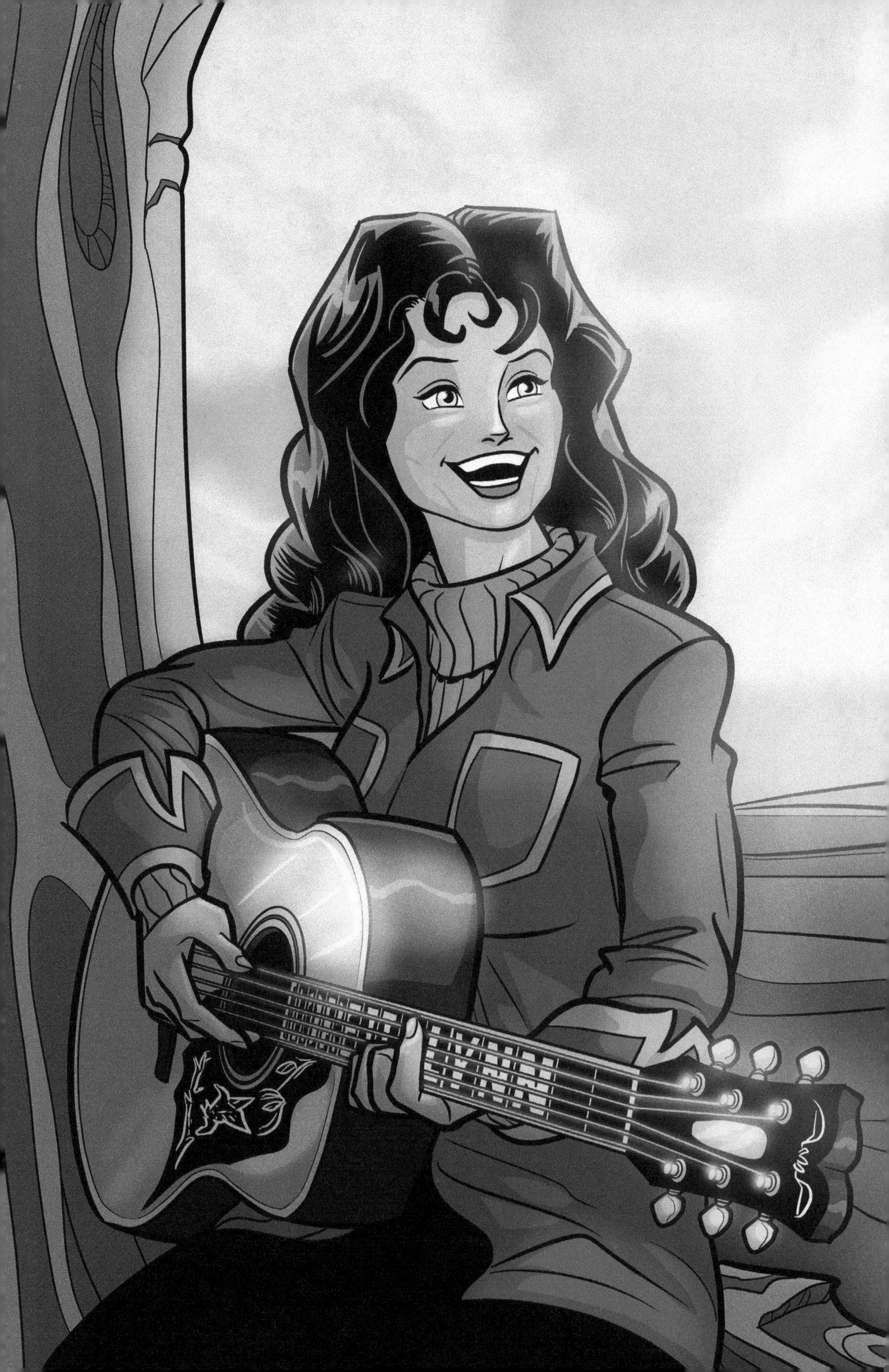
LYNN

CPSIA information can be obtained
at www.ICGtesting.com
Printed in the USA
BVHW012159131022
649153BV00043B/280

9 781956 841282